GUIDELINES FOR THE ASSESSMENT OF GENERAL DAMAGES IN PERSONAL INJURY CASES

GUIDELINES FOR THE ASSESSMENT OF GENERAL DAMAGES IN PERSONAL INJURY CASES

Eighth Edition

Compiled for the

Judicial Studies Board

by

MR JUSTICE MACKAY; MARTIN BRUFFELL, SOLICITOR;
JOHN CHERRY, QC; ALAN HUGHES, SOLICITOR;
MICHAEL TILLETT QC

Foreword by the Hon. Mr Justice Owen

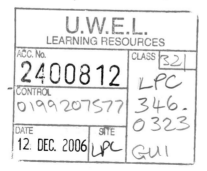
OXFORD
UNIVERSITY PRESS

OXFORD
UNIVERSITY PRESS

Great Clarendon Street, Oxford OX2 6DP

Oxford University Press is a department of the University of Oxford.
It furthers the University's objective of excellence in research, scholarship,
and education by publishing worldwide in

Oxford New York

Auckland Cape Town Dar es Salaam Hong Kong Karachi
Kuala Lumpur Madrid Melbourne Mexico City Nairobi
New Delhi Shanghai Taipei Toronto

With offices in

Argentina Austria Brazil Chile Czech Republic France Greece
Guatemala Hungary Italy Japan Poland Portugal Singapore
South Korea Switzerland Thailand Turkey Ukraine Vietnam

Oxford is a registered trade mark of Oxford University Press
in the UK and in certain other countries

Published in the United States
by Oxford University Press Inc., New York

© Judicial Studies Board, 2006

British Library Cataloguing in Publication Data

Data available

Library of Congress Cataloging in Publication Data

Guidelines for the assessment of general damages in personal injury cases / compiled for the
Judicial Studies Board by Mr Justice Mackay . . . [et al.] ; foreword by Mr Justice Owen.—8th ed.
    p. cm.
    Includes index.
    ISBN-13: 978–0–19–920757–2 (alk. paper)   1. Personal injuries—England.
2. Damages—England.   3. Personal injuries—Wales.   4. Damages—Wales.
I. Mackay, Colin, 1943–   II. Great Britain. Judicial Studies Board.
    KD1954.Z9G84 2006
    346.4293'23—dc22

2006020523

Typeset by RefineCatch Limited, Bungay, Suffolk
Printed in Great Britain
on acid-free paper by
CPI Bath Press

ISBN 0–19–920757–7   978–0–19–920757–2

1 3 5 7 9 10 8 6 4 2

Contents

Foreword by the Hon. Mr Justice Owen

I am delighted to have been asked to write the foreword for this, the eighth edition of the JSB's *Guidelines for the Assessment of General Damages in Personal Injury Cases.*

Since the publication of the first edition in 1992, this small book has been widely adopted as the starting point in negotiating levels of payment for general damages in personal injury cases.

The aim of the book has remained to report on those awards made by courts in England and Wales. In fact, it is now only in rare cases that courts make awards outside the margins reproduced in the *Guidelines.* Anecdotal evidence suggests that this is also the case in negotiated settlements— although those amounts fall outside the remit of this text.

Although amendments to the figures included in the book are therefore now largely the result of inflation, the editorial team also keeps a constant eye on the way in which the information is laid out, and makes every effort, often as the result of comments from its readership, to ensure that the breakdown of amounts under each heading is as clear as possible.

That editorial team has been led for the first time for the purposes of this edition by Colin Mackay. I am grateful to them all for the hard work that this deceptively slim volume represents.

Robert Owen

Foreword to the First Edition
by Lord Donaldson of Lymington

Paradoxical as it may seem, one of the commonest tasks of a judge sitting in a civil court is also one of the most difficult. This is the assessment of general damages for pain, suffering or loss of the amenities of life. Since no monetary award can compensate in any real sense, these damages cannot be assessed by a process of calculation. Yet whilst no two cases are ever precisely the same, justice requires that there be consistency between awards.

The solution to this dilemma has lain in using the amount of damages awarded in reported cases as guidelines or markers and seeking to slot the particular case into the framework thus provided. This is easier stated than done, because reports of the framework cases are scattered over a variety of publications and not all the awards appear, from the sometimes brief reports, to be consistent with one another. Furthermore some of the older cases are positively misleading unless account is taken of changes in the value of money and the process of revaluation is far from being an exact science.

It was against this background that the Judicial Studies Board set up a working party under the chairmanship of Judge Roger Cox to prepare 'Guidelines for the Assessment of General Damages in Personal Injury Cases'. It was not intended to represent, and does not represent, a new or different approach to the problem. Nor is it intended to be a 'ready reckoner' or in any way to fetter the individual judgment which must be brought to bear upon the unique features of each particular case. What it is intended to do, and what it does quite admirably, is to distil the conventional wisdom contained in the reported cases, to supplement it from the collective experience of the working party and to present the result in a convenient, logical and coherent form.

There can be no doubt about the practical value of this report and it has been agreed by the four Heads of Division that it shall be circulated to all judges, recorders and district judges who may be concerned with the assessment of general damages in personal injury cases. We also consider that it should be made available to the two branches of the practising profession and to any others who would be assisted by it.

Judges and practitioners will, as always, remain free to take full account of the amount of damages awarded in earlier cases, but it is hoped that with the publication of this report this will less often be necessary. They will also need to take account of cases reported after the effective date of the working party's report since that report, while to some extent providing a new base-line, is not intended to, and could not, freeze the scale of damages either absolutely or in relative terms as between different categories of loss.

May I convey my sincere congratulations to the authors upon the excellent way in which they have performed their task.

Lord Donaldson of Lymington
25 March 1992

Introduction

Following our past practice we have revised the figures in this eighth edition to take account of awards reported over the last two years and the impact of inflation. The body of data available as source material has if anything shrunk even further than has been the case in earlier years, and decisions, especially by High Court and circuit judges, on general damages are now in relative terms few and far between. There are a number of reasons for this, one of which we venture to think may be that this work itself has continued to facilitate a high number of settlements over the years and rendered unnecessary litigation over this part, at least, of a personal injury claim. If so, it has achieved its object, though there is a price to be paid—the clear danger of our work becoming self-supporting as a result.

In the case of injuries which are discrete and easily defined, we have noticed a tendency in some recent awards to divide the general damages almost into two sections, as for example: 'Loss of two front teeth JSB 7(f)(ii) £2,500; pain and suffering £1,500'. If this reflects a transparent calculation in which the suggested tariff figure is being adjusted to reflect the facts of the particular claimant's case, it is in our view a good practice. If, however, it reflects a practice of taking our figure as a form of base compensation to which a conventional amenity award should be added, it should be guarded against.

As always, the Working Party welcome comments and suggestions from all quarters, even of settlements and approved awards, though obviously we prefer the results of argued decisions. Where the former are concerned, it is useful where possible to have a breakdown of the global figure for pain, suffering and loss of amenity. Some correspondents, especially from the insurance industry, have expressed the view that we need to move towards some form of public tariff in this area of the law, and that this book should see itself as part of this process. Whatever the merits of such a proposal, that is not what this work sets out to do. We emphasise that we are not advocating the level at which we think awards ought to be made; we merely seek to record what we find are the awards being made or agreed in practice on a daily basis at all levels and in all tribunals and to ensure these keep pace with the passage of time and the impact of inflation.

As before, we have gone back two editions when updating figures, and still follow the practice on 'rounding' described in the introduction to the seventh edition.

A substantial health warning is needed in relation to Chapter 5(C)(e) to (f). The difficult question of compensation for asymptomatic pleural plaques caused by asbestos exposure is as we go to press due for consideration by the House of Lords and we have endeavoured to capture the law as we understand it to be at present. It is entirely possible that events may move so as to render this section of the work unreliable and care should be taken. We do not see it as within our remit to predict the outcome of their Lordships' study of this age-old problem, still less to presume to offer them advice as to the way they should go.

Our thanks are due to Rodger Bell for his past leadership of the Working Party, and to the JSB's coordinator Andrea Dowsett who has chivvied us along with skill and charm. She it is to whom comments, suggestions and contributions should be directed, at 9th Floor, Millbank Tower, Millbank, London SW1 4QU, or at andrea.dowsett@jsb.gsi.gov.uk.

The figures in this edition are expressed as at June 2006.

1

Injuries Involving Paralysis

(a) Quadriplegia   £188,250 to £235,000

The level of the award within the bracket will be affected by the following considerations:

   (i)   the extent of any residual movement;

  (ii)   the presence and extent of pain;

 (iii)   depression;

 (iv)   age and life expectancy.

The top of the bracket will be appropriate only where there is significant effect on senses or ability to communicate. It will also often involve significant brain damage: see 2(A)(a).

(b) Paraplegia   £127,250 to £165,500

The level of the award within the bracket will be affected by the following considerations:

   (i)   the presence and extent of pain;

  (ii)   the degree of independence;

 (iii)   depression;

 (iv)   age and life expectancy.

The presence of increasing paralysis or the degree of risk that this will occur, for example, from syringomyelia, might take the case above this bracket. The latter might be the subject of a provisional damages order.

2

Head Injuries

(A) BRAIN DAMAGE

(a) Very Severe Brain Damage   £165,500 to £235,000

In cases at the top of this bracket the injured person will have a degree of insight. There may be some ability to follow basic commands, recovery of eye opening and return of sleep and waking patterns and postural reflex movement. There will be little, if any, evidence of meaningful response to environment, little or no language function, double incontinence and the need for full-time nursing care.

The level of the award within the bracket will be affected by:

  (i)   the degree of insight;

  (ii) life expectancy;

  (iii) the extent of physical limitations.

The top of the bracket will be appropriate only where there is significant effect on the senses and severe physical limitation.

Where there is a persistent vegetative state and/or death occurs very soon after the injuries were suffered and there has been no awareness by the injured person of his or her condition the award will be solely for loss of amenity and will fall substantially below the above bracket.

(b) Moderately Severe Brain Injury £127,250 to £165,500

The injured person will be very seriously disabled. There will be substantial dependence on others and a need for constant professional and other care. Disabilities may be physical, for example, limb paralysis, or cognitive, with marked impairment of intellect and personality. Cases otherwise within (a) above may fall into this bracket if life expectancy has been greatly reduced.

The level of the award within the bracket will be affected by the following considerations:

  (i)   the degree of insight;

  (ii) life expectancy;

  (iii) the extent of physical limitations;

  (iv) the degree of dependence on others;

  (v)   ability to communicate;

  (vi) behavioural abnormality;

  (vii) epilepsy or a significant risk of epilepsy (unless a provisional damages order provides for this risk).

(c) Moderate Brain Damage

This category is distinguished from (b) by the fact that the degree of dependence is markedly lower.

(i) Cases in which there is moderate to severe intellectual deficit, a personality change, an effect on sight, speech and senses with a significant risk of epilepsy and no prospect of employment. £87,500 to £127,250

(ii) Cases in which there is a moderate to modest intellectual deficit, the ability to work is greatly reduced if not removed and there is some risk of epilepsy (unless a provisional damages order provides for this risk). £52,950 to £87,500

(iii) Cases in which concentration and memory are affected, the ability to work is reduced, where there is a small risk of epilepsy and any dependence on others is very limited. £25,000 to £52,950

(d) Minor Brain Damage £9,000 to £25,000

In these cases the injured person will have made a good recovery and will be able to take part in normal social life and to return to work. There may not have been a restoration of all normal functions so there may still be persisting problems such as poor concentration and memory or disinhibition of mood, which may interfere with lifestyle, leisure activities and future work prospects. At the top of this bracket there may be a small risk of epilepsy.

The level of the award within the bracket will be affected by:

(i) the extent and severity of the initial injury;

(ii) the extent of any continuing, and possibly permanent, disability;

(iii) the extent of any personality change;

(iv) depression.

(B) Minor Head Injury   £1,300 to £7,425

In these cases brain damage, if any, will have been minimal.

The level of the award will be affected by the following considerations:

   (i)   the severity of the initial injury;

   (ii)   the period taken to recover from any symptoms;

   (iii)   the extent of continuing symptoms;

   (iv)   the presence or absence of headaches.

The bottom of the bracket will reflect full recovery within a few weeks.

(C) Epilepsy

(a) **Established Grand Mal**   £58,500 to £87,500

(b) **Established Petit Mal**   £32,000 to £76,350

The level of the award within these brackets will be affected by the following factors:

   (i)   whether attacks are successfully controlled by medication and the extent to which the need for medication is likely to persist;

   (ii)   the extent to which the appreciation of life is blunted by such medication;

   (iii)   the effect on working and/or social life;

(iv) the existence of associated behavioural problems;

(v) the prognosis.

(c) Other Epileptic Conditions   £6,100 to £15,250

Cases where there are one or two discrete epileptic episodes, or a temporary resurgence of epilepsy, but there is no risk of further recurrence beyond that applicable to the population at large. The level of the award within the bracket will be affected by the extent of any consequences of the attacks on, for example, education, sporting activities, working and social life, and their duration.

3

Psychiatric Damage

In part (A) of this chapter some of the brackets contain an element of compensation for post-traumatic stress disorder. This is of course not a universal feature of cases of psychiatric injury and hence a number of the awards upon which the brackets are based did not reflect it. Where it does figure any award will tend towards the upper end of the bracket. Cases where post-traumatic stress disorder is the sole psychiatric condition are dealt with in part (B) of this chapter. Where cases arise out of sexual and/or physical abuse in breach of parental, family or other trust, involving victims who are young and/or vulnerable, awards will tend to be at the upper end of the relevant bracket to take into account (A)(vii) below.

Part (C) of this chapter deals with various conditions under the generic heading 'Chronic Pain'. These are cases where there are symptoms of pain without any, or any commensurate, organic basis. Questions of causation inevitably arise in such cases, but it is not the function of the Guidelines to consider them, and the figures given in the various sections are on the basis that causation is established. While the conditions dealt with in part (C) do not necessarily arise out of psychiatric injury, they are dealt with here partly because they almost always include an element of psychological damage and partly for the convenience of users of the Guidelines, because symptoms caused by these conditions can affect a variety of areas of an injured person's anatomy. The figures given include compensation for any physical injury and for any physical disability resulting from the chronic pain.

(A) Psychiatric Damage Generally

The factors to be taken into account in valuing claims of this nature are as follows:

(i) the injured person's ability to cope with life and work;

(ii) the effect on the injured person's relationships with family, friends and those with whom he or she comes into contact;

(iii) the extent to which treatment would be successful;

(iv) future vulnerability;

(v) prognosis;

(vi) whether medical help has been sought;

(vii) (a) whether the injury results from sexual and/or physical abuse and/or breach of trust;

(b) if so, the nature of the relationship between victim and abuser, the nature of the abuse, its duration and the symptoms caused by it.

(a) Severe   £32,000 to £67,200

In these cases the injured person will have marked problems with respect to factors (i) to (iv) above and the prognosis will be very poor.

(b) Moderately Severe   £11,200 to £32,000

In these cases there will be significant problems associated with factors (i) to (iv) above but the prognosis will be much more optimistic than in (a) above. While there are awards which support both extremes of this bracket, the majority are somewhere near the middle of the bracket. Cases of work-related stress resulting in a permanent or long-standing disability preventing a return to comparable employment would appear to come within this category.

(c) Moderate   £3,450 to £11,200

While there may have been the sort of problems associated with factors (i) to (iv) above there will have been marked improvement by trial and the prognosis will be good.

(d) Minor   £840 to £3,450

The level of the award will take into consideration the length of the period of disability and the extent to which daily activities and sleep were affected. Awards have been made below this bracket in cases of temporary 'anxiety'.

(B) Post-Traumatic Stress Disorder

Cases within this category are exclusively those where there is a specific diagnosis of a reactive psychiatric disorder in which characteristic symptoms are displayed following a psychologically distressing event which causes intense fear, helplessness and horror. The guidelines below have been compiled by reference to cases which variously reflect the criteria established in the 4th edition of *Diagnostic and Statistical Manual of Mental Disorders* (DSM-IV-TR). The symptoms affect basic functions such as breathing, pulse rate and bowel and/or bladder control. They also involve persistent re-experience of the relevant event, difficulty in controlling temper, in concentrating and sleeping, and exaggerated startle response.

(a) Severe   £36,650 to £58,500

Such cases will involve permanent effects which prevent the injured person from working at all or at least from functioning at anything approaching the pre-trauma level. All aspects of the life of the injured person will be badly affected.

(b) Moderately Severe   £13,500 to £33,800

This category is distinct from (a) above because of the better prognosis which will be for some recovery with professional help. However, the effects are still likely to cause significant disability for the foreseeable future. While there are awards which support both extremes of this bracket, the majority are between £20,000 and £25,000.

(c) Moderate   £4,825 to £13,500

In these cases the injured person will have largely recovered and any continuing effects will not be grossly disabling.

(d) Minor   £2,300 to £4,825

In these cases a virtually full recovery will have been made within one to two years and only minor symptoms will persist over any longer period.

(C) CHRONIC PAIN

(a) **Chronic Pain Syndrome**

    (i)   Severe   **£24,450 to £37,150**

    (ii)   Moderate   **£6,350 to £19,100**

(b) **Fibromyalgia**   **£19,850 to £37,150**

(c) **Chronic Fatigue Syndrome**   **In the region of £28,750**

(d) **Reflex Sympathetic Dystrophy**
     (Also called complex regional pain syndrome)

    (i)   Severe   **£29,750 to £58,500**

    (ii)   Moderate   **£14,750 to £22,400**

(e) **Somatoform Disorder**   **In the region of £26,500**

4

Injuries Affecting the Senses

(A) Injuries Affecting Sight

(a) Total Blindness and Deafness
In the region of
£235,000

Such cases must be considered as ranking with the most devastating injuries.

(b) Total Blindness
In the region of
£155,250

(c) Loss of Sight in One Eye with Reduced Vision in the Remaining Eye

    (i)   Where there is serious risk of further deterioration in the remaining eye, going beyond some risk of sympathetic ophthalmia.
£56,000 to £104,500

    (ii)   Where there is reduced vision in the remaining eye and/or additional problems such as double vision.
£37,150 to £61,500

(d) Total Loss of One Eye
£32,000 to £38,175

The level of the award within the bracket will depend on age and cosmetic effect.

(e) **Complete Loss of Sight in One Eye** £28,750 to £32,000

This award takes account of some risk of sympathetic ophthalmia. The upper end of the bracket
is appropriate where there is scarring in the
region of the eye which is not sufficiently serious
to merit a separate award.

(f) Cases of serious but incomplete loss of vision in
one eye without significant risk of loss or reduction of vision in the remaining eye, or where
there is constant double vision. £13,750 to £22,650

(g) Minor but permanent impairment of vision in
one eye, including cases where there is some
double vision, which may not be constant. £7,375 to £12,200

(h) **Minor Eye Injuries** £2,300 to £5,100

In this bracket fall cases of minor injuries, such
as being struck in the eye, exposure to fumes
including smoke, or being splashed by liquids,
causing initial pain and some temporary interference with vision.

(i) **Transient Eye Injuries** £1,300 to £2,300

In these cases the injured person will have
recovered completely within a few weeks.

(B) DEAFNESS

The word 'deafness' is used to embrace total and
partial hearing loss. In assessing awards for
hearing loss regard must be had to the following:

(i)   whether the injury is one that has an immediate effect, allowing no opportunity to adapt, or whether it occurred over a period of time, as in noise exposure cases;

(ii) whether the injury or disability is one which the injured person suffered at an early age so that it has had or will have an effect on his or her speech, or is one that is suffered in later life;

(iii) whether the injury or disability affects balance;

(iv) in cases of noise-induced hearing loss (NIHL) age is of particular relevance as noted in paragraph (d) below.

(a) Total Deafness and Loss of Speech   £63,625 to £81,500

Such cases arise, for example, where deafness has occurred at an early age (for example, rubella infection) so as to prevent or seriously to affect the development of normal speech.

(b) Total Deafness   £52,950 to £63,625

The lower end of the bracket is appropriate for cases where there is no speech deficit or tinnitus. The higher end is appropriate for cases involving both of these.

(c) Total Loss of Hearing in One Ear   £18,325 to £26,500

Cases will tend towards the higher end of the bracket where there are associated problems, such as tinnitus, dizziness or headaches.

(d) Partial Hearing Loss/Tinnitus

This category covers the bulk of deafness cases which usually result from exposure to noise over a prolonged period. The disability is not to be judged simply by the degree of hearing loss; there is often a degree of tinnitus present. Age is particularly relevant because impairment of hearing affects most people in the fullness of time and impacts both upon causation and upon valuation.

(i)	Severe tinnitus/hearing loss.	£17,300 to £26,500
(ii)	Moderate tinnitus/hearing loss.	£8,650 to £17,300
(iii)	Mild tinnitus with some hearing loss.	£7,375 to £8,650
(iv)	Slight or occasional tinnitus with slight hearing loss.	£4,300 to £7,375

(C) IMPAIRMENT OF TASTE AND SMELL

(a) **Total Loss of Taste and Smell**   **In the region of £22,650**

(b) **Total Loss of Smell and Significant Loss of Taste**   **£19,100 to £22,650**

It must be remembered that in nearly all cases of loss of smell there is some impairment of taste. Such cases fall into the next bracket.

(c) **Loss of Smell**   **£14,500 to £19,100**

(d) **Loss of Taste**   **£11,200 to £14,500**

5

Injuries to Internal Organs

(A) CHEST INJURIES

This is a specially difficult area because the majority of awards relate to industrial *disease* (see (B) below) as distinct from traumatic *injury*. Cases of traumatic damage to, or loss of, a lung are comparatively rare: the range is as wide as £1,300 to £87,500.

The levels of awards within the brackets set out below will be affected by:

(i)   age and gender;

(ii) scarring;

(iii) the effect on the capacity to work and enjoy life;

(iv) the effect on life expectancy.

(a) The worst type of case will be of total removal of one lung and/or serious heart damage with serious and prolonged pain and suffering and permanent significant scarring.   **£58,500 to £87,500**

(b) Traumatic injury to chest, lung(s) and/or heart causing permanent damage, impairment of

function, physical disability and reduction of life
expectancy. £38,175 to £58,500

(c) Damage to chest and lung(s) causing some continuing disability. £18,325 to £32,000

(d) A relatively simple injury (such as a single
penetrating wound) causing some permanent
damage to tissue but with no significant long-
term effect on lung function. £7,375 to £10,500

(e) Toxic fume/smoke inhalation, leaving some residual damage, not serious enough to interfere
permanently with lung function. £3,175 to £7,375

(f) Injuries leading to collapsed lungs from which a
full and uncomplicated recovery is made. £1,300 to £3,175

(g) Fractures of ribs, causing serious pain and disability over a period of weeks only. Up to £2,300

(B) Lung Disease

The level of the appropriate award for lung
disease necessarily, and often principally, reflects
the prognosis for what is frequently a worsening
condition and/or the risk of the development of
secondary sequelae.

Most of the reported cases are of asbestos-related
disease (as to which see (C) below) but, save for
asthma (which is also dealt with separately in (D)
below), the brackets set out are intended to
encompass all other lung disease cases irrespect-
ive of causation. In many cases falling under this
head provisional awards will be appropriate. At
the upper end of the range where serious disabling consequences will already be present and the
prognosis is likely to be relatively clear such an
award may not be appropriate. Furthermore, in

some cases awards may be enhanced where classifiable psychiatric illness is present.

(a) For a young person with serious disability where there is a probability of progressive worsening leading to premature death.

£58,500 to £79,000

(b) Lung cancer (typically in an older person) causing severe pain and impairment both of function and of quality of life. The duration of pain and suffering accounts for variations within this bracket. See also paragraph (C)(b) below.

£45,800 to £58,500

(c) Disease, e.g., emphysema, causing significant and worsening lung function and impairment of breathing, prolonged and frequent coughing, sleep disturbance and restriction of physical activity and employment.

£32,000 to £46,300

(d) Breathing difficulties (short of disabling breathlessness) requiring fairly frequent use of an inhaler; where there is inability to tolerate a smoky environment and an uncertain prognosis but already significant effect on social and working life.

£18,325 to £32,000

(e) Bronchitis and wheezing not causing serious symptoms; little or no serious or permanent effect on working or social life; varying levels of anxiety about the future.

£12,200 to £18,325

(f) Some slight breathlessness with no effect on working life and the likelihood of substantial and permanent recovery within a few years of the exposure to the cause or the aggravation of an existing condition.

£6,100 to £12,200

(g) Provisional awards for cases otherwise falling within (f), or the least serious cases within (e) where the provisional award excludes any risk of malignancy.

£3,175 to £6,100

(h) Temporary aggravation of bronchitis or other chest problems resolving within a very few months. **£1,300 to £3,175**

(C) ASBESTOS-RELATED DISEASE

Mesothelioma, lung cancer and asbestosis are the most serious of these. Mesothelioma is typically of shorter duration than either of the other two and often proves fatal within a matter of months from first diagnosis. Lung cancer and asbestosis are likely to have a fatal outcome but the symptoms often endure for several years. Where damages for pleural plaques are concerned, note that entitlement to and quantification of damages are under appeal to the House of Lords at the date of publication.

(a) Mesothelioma causing severe pain and impairment of both function and quality of life. This may be of the pleura (the lung lining) or of the peritoneum (the lining of the abdominal cavity); the latter being typically more painful. The duration of pain and suffering accounts for variations within this bracket. For periods of up to 18 months, awards in the bottom half of the bracket may be appropriate; for longer periods of four years or more, an award at the top end. **£47,850 to £74,300**

(b) Lung cancer, again a disease proving fatal in most cases, the symptoms of which may not be as painful as those of mesothelioma, but more protracted. See also paragraph (B)(b) above. **£45,800 to £58,500**

(c) Asbestosis, causing impairment of the extremities of the lungs so that oxygen uptake to the blood stream is reduced. In the early stages the disease may be symptomless but progresses to cause severe breathlessness. Mobility is likely to become seriously impaired and quality of life

reduced. Respiratory disability of between 10
and 20 per cent will probably attract an award in
the region of £40,750.   **£28,000 to £61,500**

(d) Pleural thickening, typically causing progressive
symptoms of breathlessness by inhibiting expan-
sion of the lungs (the so-called *cuirasse* restriction). Disease may gradually progress to cause
more serious respiratory disability.   **£22,400 to £45,800**

(e) Pleural plaques, being localised areas of pleural
thickening, do not normally cause any symptoms. May be accompanied by psychological
injury causing disability.   **£6,100 to £7,125**

(f) Provisional awards for cases otherwise falling
within (e) or the least serious cases within (d)
where the provisional award excludes any risk of
the development of mesothelioma, lung or other
cancer or asbestosis.   **£4,000 to £6,100**

(D) Asthma

(a) Severe and permanent disabling asthma, causing
prolonged and regular coughing, disturbance of
sleep, severe impairment of physical activity and
enjoyment of life and where employment pros-
pects, if any, are grossly restricted.   **£25,000 to £38,175**

(b) Chronic asthma causing breathing difficulties,
the need to use an inhaler from time to time and
restriction of employment prospects, with
uncertain prognosis.   **£15,250 to £25,000**

(c) Bronchitis and wheezing, affecting working or
social life, with the likelihood of substantial
recovery within a few years of the exposure to
the cause.   **£11,200 to £15,250**

(d) Relatively mild asthma-like symptoms often resulting, for instance, from exposure to harmful irritating vapour.   **£6,100 to £11,200**

(e) Mild asthma, bronchitis, colds and chest problems (usually resulting from unfit housing or similar exposure, particularly in cases of young children) treated by a general practitioner and resolving within a few months.   **Up to £3,000**

(E) Reproductive System: Male

(a) Impotence

    (i) Total impotence and loss of sexual function and sterility in the case of a young man.   **In the region of £86,500**

The level of the award will depend on:

       (1) age;

       (2) psychological reaction and the effect on social and domestic life.

    (ii) Impotence which is likely to be permanent, in the case of a middle-aged man with children.   **£25,000 to £46,300**

(b) Cases of sterility usually fall into one of two categories: surgical, chemical and disease cases (which involve no traumatic injury or scarring) and traumatic injuries (frequently caused by assaults) which are often aggravated by scarring.

    (i) The most serious cases merit awards approaching   **£81,500**

    (ii) The bottom of the range is the case of the much older man and merits an award of about   **£10,700**

(c) An uncomplicated case of sterility without impotence and without any aggravating features for a young man without children. **£32,800 to £41,250**

(d) A similar case but involving a family man who might have intended to have more children. **£13,750 to £18,100**

(e) Cases where the sterility amounts to little more than an 'insult'. **In the region of £3,800**

(F) REPRODUCTIVE SYSTEM: FEMALE

The level of awards in this area will typically depend on:

(i) whether or not the affected woman already has children and/or whether the intended family was complete;

(ii) scarring;

(iii) depression or psychological scarring;

(iv) whether a foetus was aborted.

(a) Infertility whether by reason of injury or disease, with severe depression and anxiety, pain and scarring. **£67,200 to £98,500**

(b) Infertility without any medical complication and where the injured person already has children. The upper end of the bracket is appropriate in cases where there is significant psychological damage. **£10,500 to £21,350**

(c) Infertility where the injured person would not have had children in any event (for example, because of age). **£3,800 to £7,425**

(d) Failed sterilisation leading to unwanted pregnancy where there is no serious psychological impact or depression. **In the region of £5,850**

(G) Digestive System

The risk of associated damage to the reproductive organs is frequently encountered in cases of this nature and requires separate consideration.

(a) Damage Resulting from Traumatic Injury

(i) Severe damage with continuing pain and discomfort. £25,000 to £36,125

(ii) Serious non-penetrating injury causing long-standing or permanent complications, for example, severe indigestion, aggravated by physical strain. £9,700 to £16,300

(iii) Penetrating stab wounds or industrial laceration or serious seat-belt pressure cases. £3,800 to £7,375

(b) Illness/Damage Resulting from Non-traumatic Injury, e.g. Food Poisoning

There will be a marked distinction between those, comparatively rare, cases having a long-standing or even permanent effect on quality of life and those in which the only continuing symptoms may be allergy to specific foods and the attendant risk of short-term illness.

(i) Severe toxicosis causing serious acute pain, vomiting, diarrhoea and fever, requiring hospital admission for some days or weeks and some continuing incontinence, haemorrhoids and irritable bowel syndrome, having a significant impact on ability to work and enjoyment of life. £22,400 to £30,500

(ii) Serious but short-lived food poisoning, diarrhoea and vomiting diminishing over two to four weeks with some remaining discomfort and disturbance of bowel function and impact on sex life and enjoyment of food over a few years. Any such symptoms having these consequences and lasting for longer, even indefinitely, are likely to merit an award between the top of this bracket and the bottom of the bracket in (i) above. **£5,600 to £11,200**

(iii) Food poisoning causing significant discomfort, stomach cramps, alteration of bowel function and fatigue. Hospital admission for some days with symptoms lasting for a few weeks but complete recovery within a year or two. **£2,300 to £5,600**

(iv) Varying degrees of disabling pain, cramps and diarrhoea continuing for some days or weeks. **£550 to £2,300**

(H) KIDNEY

(a) Serious and permanent damage to or loss of both kidneys. **£98,500 to £122,000**

(b) Where there is a significant risk of future urinary tract infection or other total loss of natural kidney function. **Up to £37,150**

Such cases will invariably carry with them substantial future medical expenses, which in this field are particularly high.

(c) Loss of one kidney with no damage to the other. **£18,100 to £25,000**

(I) BOWELS

(a) Total loss of natural function and dependence on colostomy, depending on age. **Up to £87,500**

(b) Severe abdominal injury causing impairment of function and often necessitating temporary colostomy (leaving disfiguring scars) and/or restriction on employment and on diet. **£26,000 to £40,750**

(c) Penetrating injuries causing some permanent damage but with an eventual return to natural function and control. **£7,375 to £14,000**

(J) BLADDER

It is perhaps surprising that awards in cases of loss of bladder function have often been higher than awards for injury to the bowels. This is probably because bladder injuries frequently result from carcinogenic exposure. The reported decisions are seriously out of date and merely increasing them to reflect inflation may be misleading.

(a) Complete loss of function and control. **Up to £81,500**

(b) Serious impairment of control with some pain and incontinence. **£37,150 to £46,300**

(c) Where there has been almost a complete recovery but some fairly long-term interference with natural function. **£13,500 to £18,100**

The cancer risk cases still occupy a special category and can properly attract awards at the top of the ranges even where natural function continues for the time being. However, these cases will now more appropriately be dealt with by provisional awards at a low level (£5,600) unless the foreseeable outcome is clear. Once the prognosis is firm and reliable the award will reflect any loss of life expectancy, the level of continuing pain and suffering and most significantly the extent to which the injured person has to live with the knowledge of the consequences which his or her death will have for others. The appropriate award for the middle-aged family man or woman whose life expectancy is reduced by 15 or 20 years is £30,500 to £44,500.

(K) SPLEEN

(a) Loss of spleen where there is continuing risk of internal infection and disorders due to the damage to the immune system.   **£12,200 to £15,250**

(b) Where the above risks are not present or are minimal.   **£2,550 to £5,100**

(L) HERNIA

(a) Continuing pain and/or limitation on physical activities, sport or employment, after repair.   **£8,650 to £14,000**

(b) Direct (where there was no pre-existing weakness) inguinal hernia, with some risk of recurrence, after repair.   **£4,000 to £5,350**

(c) Uncomplicated indirect inguinal hernia, possibly repaired, and with no other associated abdominal injury or damage.   **£2,000 to £4,300**

6

Orthopaedic Injuries

(A) Neck Injuries

There is a very wide range of neck injuries. Many are found in conjunction with back and shoulder problems.

At the highest level are injuries which shatter life and leave claimants very severely disabled. These may have a value of up to £86,500.

At the lowest level, claimants may suffer a minor strain, may not have time off work, and may suffer symptoms for a few weeks, justifying as little as £750.

(a) Severe

(i) Neck injury associated with incomplete paraplegia or resulting in permanent spastic quadriparesis or where the injured person, despite wearing a collar 24 hours a day for a period of years, still has little or no movement in the neck and suffers severe headaches which have proved intractable.   **In the region of £86,500**

(ii) Injuries which give rise to disabilities which fall short of those in (a)(i) above but which are of considerable severity; for example, permanent damage to the brachial plexus.

£38,175 to £76,350

(iii) Injuries causing severe damage to soft tissues and/or ruptured tendons. They result in significant disability of a permanent nature. The precise award depends on the length of time during which the most serious symptoms are ameliorated, and on the prognosis.

In the region of £32,000

(iv) Injuries such as fractures or dislocations which cause severe immediate symptoms and which may necessitate spinal fusion. They leave markedly impaired function or vulnerability to further trauma, and some limitation of activities.

£14,500 to £19,100

(b) Moderate

(i) Cases involving whiplash or wrenching-type injury and disc lesion of the more severe type resulting in cervical spondylosis, serious limitation of movement, permanent or recurring pain, stiffness or discomfort and the possible need for further surgery or increased vulnerability to further trauma.

£8,150 to £14,500

(ii) Injuries which may have exacerbated or accelerated some pre-existing unrelated condition. There will have been a complete recovery or recovery to 'nuisance' level from the effects of the accident within a few years. This bracket will also apply to moderate whiplash injuries where the period of recovery has been fairly protracted and where there remains an increased vulnerability to further trauma.

£4,575 to £8,150

(c) Minor

Minor soft tissue and whiplash injuries and the like where symptoms are moderate:

(i) and a full recovery takes place within about two years; **£2,550 to £4,575**

(ii) with a full recovery between a few weeks and a year. **£750 to £2,550**

(B) Back Injuries

Relatively few back injuries which do not give rise to paralysis command awards above about £25,000. In those that do there are special features.

(a) Severe

(i) Cases of the most severe injury which do not involve paralysis but where there may be very serious consequences not normally found in cases of back injury, such as impotence or double incontinence. **£58,500 to £98,500**

(ii) Cases which have special features taking them outside any lower bracket applicable to orthopaedic injury to the back. Such features include impaired bladder and bowel function, severe sexual difficulties and unsightly scarring and the possibility of future surgery. **In the region of £46,300**

(iii) Cases of disc lesions or fractures of discs or of vertebral bodies where, despite treatment, there remain disabilities such as continuing severe pain and discomfort, impaired agility, impaired sexual function,

depression, personality change, alcohol-
ism, unemployability and the risk of arth-
ritis.   £22,650 to £40,750

(b) Moderate

(i)   Cases where any residual disability is of
      less severity than that in (a)(iii) above. The
      bracket contains a wide variety of injuries.
      Examples are a case of a crush fracture of
      the lumbar vertebrae where there is a sub-
      stantial risk of osteoarthritis and constant
      pain and discomfort with impairment of
      sexual function; that of a traumatic
      spondylolisthesis with continuous pain
      and a probability that spinal fusion will be
      necessary; or that of a prolapsed inter-
      vertebral disc with substantial acceleration
      of back degeneration.   £16,300 to £22,650

(ii) Many frequently encountered injuries to
      the back such as disturbance of ligaments
      and muscles giving rise to backache, soft
      tissue injuries resulting in exacerbation of
      an existing back condition or prolapsed
      discs necessitating laminectomy or result-
      ing in repeated relapses. The precise figure
      depends upon the severity of the original
      injury and/or whether there is some per-
      manent or chronic disability.   £7,125 to £16,300

(c) Minor

Strains, sprains, disc prolapses and soft tissue
injuries from which a full recovery or recovery to
'nuisance' level has been made without surgery:

(i)   within about five years;   £4,575 to £7,125

(ii) within about two years.   Up to £4,575

(C) Shoulder Injuries

(a) Severe
£11,200 to £28,000

Often associated with neck injuries and involving damage to the brachial plexus (see (A)(a)(ii)) resulting in significant disability.

(b) Serious
£7,375 to £11,200

Dislocation of the shoulder and damage to the lower part of the brachial plexus causing pain in shoulder and neck, aching in elbow, sensory symptoms in the forearm and hand, and weakness of grip.

(c) Moderate
£4,575 to £7,375

Frozen shoulder with limitation of movement and discomfort with symptoms persisting for about two years.

(d) Minor

Soft tissue injury to shoulder with considerable pain but almost complete recovery:

   (i) in less than two years;
£2,550 to £4,575

   (ii) within a year.
Up to £2,550

(e) Fracture of Clavicle
£3,000 to £7,125

The level of the award will depend on extent of fracture, level of disability, residual symptoms, and whether temporary or permanent, and whether union is anatomically displaced.

(D) Injuries to the Pelvis and Hips

The most serious of injuries to the pelvis and hip can be as devastating as a leg amputation and accordingly will attract a similar award of damages. Such cases apart, the upper limit for these injuries will generally be in the region of £38,175. Cases where there are specific sequelae of exceptional severity would call for a higher award.

(a) Severe

(i) Extensive fractures of the pelvis involving, for example, dislocation of a low back joint and a ruptured bladder, or a hip injury resulting in spondylolisthesis of a low back joint with intolerable pain and necessitating spinal fusion. Inevitably there will be substantial residual disabilities such as a complicated arthrodesis with resulting lack of bladder and bowel control, sexual dysfunction or hip deformity making the use of a calliper essential; or may present difficulties for natural delivery. £46,300 to £76,350

(ii) Injuries only a little less severe than in (a)(i) above but with particular distinguishing features lifting them above any lower bracket. Examples are: (a) fracture dislocation of the pelvis involving both ischial and pubic rami and resulting in impotence; or (b) traumatic myositis ossificans with formation of ectopic bone around the hip. £36,125 to £46,300

(iii) Many injuries fall within this bracket: a fracture of the acetabulum leading to degenerative changes and leg instability requiring an osteotomy and the likelihood of hip replacement surgery in the future; the fracture of an arthritic femur or hip necessitating hip replacement; or a fracture resulting in a hip replacement which is only partially successful so that there is a clear risk of the need for revision surgery.   £22,650 to £30,500

(b) Moderate   £15,500 to £22,650

Significant injury to the pelvis or hip but any permanent disability is not major and any future risk not great.

(c) Injuries of Limited Severity   £7,375 to £15,500

These cases may involve hip replacement. Where it has been carried out wholly successfully the award will tend to the top of the bracket, but the bracket also includes cases where hip replacement may be necessary in the foreseeable future.

(d) Lesser Injuries

  (i)   Cases where despite significant injury there is little or no residual disability.   £2,175 to £7,375

  (ii) Minor injuries with complete recovery.   Up to £2,175

(E) Amputation of Arms

(a) Loss of Both Arms   £140,500 to £174,500

There is no recent case to offer guidance but the effect of such an injury is to reduce a person with full awareness to a state of considerable helplessness.

(b) Loss of One Arm

(i)	Arm Amputated at the Shoulder	Not less than £79,000
(ii)	Above-elbow Amputation	£63,625 to £76,350

A shorter stump may create difficulties in the use of a prosthesis. This will make the level of the award towards the top end of the bracket. Amputation through the elbow will normally produce an award at the bottom end of the bracket.

(iii)	Below-elbow Amputation	£56,000 to £63,625

Amputation through the forearm with residual severe organic and phantom pains would attract an award at the top end of the bracket.

The value of such an injury depends upon:

(i) whether the amputation is above or below the elbow. The loss of the additional joint adds greatly to the disability;

(ii) whether or not the amputation was of the dominant arm;

(iii) the intensity of any phantom pains.

(F) OTHER ARM INJURIES

(a) Severe Injuries	£56,000 to £76,350

Injuries which fall short of amputation but which are extremely serious and leave the injured person little better off than if the arm had been lost; for example, a serious brachial plexus injury.

(b) **Injuries resulting in Permanent and
     Substantial Disablement**   £22,650 to £34,850

Serious fractures of one or both forearms where
there is significant permanent residual disability
whether functional or cosmetic.

(c) **Less Severe Injury**   £11,200 to £22,650

While there will have been significant disabilities, a substantial degree of recovery will
have taken place or will be expected.

(d) **Simple Fractures of the Forearm**   £3,800 to £11,200

Uncomplicated fractures of the radius and/or
ulna with a complete recovery within a short
time would justify an award of £3,700. Injuries
resulting in modest residual disability or deformity would merit an award towards the upper end
of this bracket.

(G) INJURIES TO THE ELBOW

(a) **A Severely Disabling Injury**   £22,650 to £32,000

(b) **Less Severe Injuries**   £9,150 to £18,325

Injuries causing impairment of function but not
involving major surgery or significant disability.

(c) **Moderate or Minor Injury**   Up to £7,375

Most elbow injuries fall into this category. They
comprise simple fractures, tennis elbow syndrome and lacerations; i.e., those injuries which

cause no permanent damage and do not result in any permanent impairment of function.

(H) WRIST INJURIES

(a) Injuries resulting in complete loss of function in the wrist, for example, where an arthrodesis has been performed.

£27,750 to £34,850

(b) Injury resulting in significant permanent disability, but where some useful movement remains.

£14,250 to £22,650

(c) Less severe injuries where these still result in some permanent disability as, for example, a degree of persisting pain and stiffness.

£7,375 to £14,250

(d) An uncomplicated Colles' fracture.

In the region of £4,300

(e) Very minor undisplaced or minimally displaced fractures and the like necessitating application of plaster or bandage for a matter of weeks and a full or virtual recovery within a matter of months.

£2,000 to £2,800

Where recovery from fracture or soft tissue injury takes longer but is complete, the award will rarely exceed £5,850.

(I) HAND INJURIES

The hands are cosmetically and functionally the most important component parts of the upper limbs. The loss of a hand is valued not far short of the amount which would be awarded for the loss of the arm itself. The upper end of any bracket will generally be appropriate where the injury is to the dominant hand.

(a) **Total or Effective Loss of Both Hands** £81,500 to £117,000

Serious injury resulting in extensive damage to both hands such as to render them little more than useless will justify an award of £80,000 or more. The top of the bracket is applicable where no effective prosthesis can be used.

(b) **Serious Damage to Both Hands** £32,000 to £49,350

Such injuries will have given rise to permanent cosmetic disability and significant loss of function.

(c) **Total or Effective Loss of One Hand** £56,000 to £63,625

This bracket will apply to a hand which was crushed and thereafter surgically amputated or where all fingers and most of the palm have been traumatically amputated. The upper end of the bracket is indicated where the hand so damaged was the dominant one.

(d) **Amputation of Index and Middle and/or Ring Fingers** £36,125 to £52,950

The hand will have been rendered of very little use and such grip as remains will be exceedingly weak.

(e) **Serious Hand Injuries** £16,800 to £36,125

Such injuries will, for example, have reduced the hand to about 50 per cent capacity. Included would be cases where several fingers have been amputated but rejoined to the hand leaving it clawed, clumsy and unsightly, or amputation of some fingers together with part of the palm resulting in gross diminution of grip and dexterity and gross cosmetic disfigurement.

(f) Less Serious Hand Injury   £8,400 to £16,800

Such as a severe crush injury resulting in significantly impaired function without future surgery
or despite operative treatment undergone.

(g) Moderate Hand Injury   £3,800 to £7,625

Crush injuries, penetrating wounds, soft tissue
type and deep lacerations. The top of the bracket
would be appropriate where surgery has failed
and permanent disability remains.

(h) Minor Hand Injuries   £500 to £2,550

Injuries similar to but less serious than (g) above
with recovery within a few months.

(i) Severe Fractures to Fingers   Up to £21,350

These may lead to partial amputations and result
in deformity, impairment of grip, reduced mech-
anical function and disturbed sensation.

(j) Total Loss of Index Finger   In the region of £10,700

(k) Partial Loss of Index Finger   £7,125 to £10,700

This bracket also covers cases of injury to the
index finger giving rise to disfigurement and
impairment of grip or dexterity.

(l) Fracture of Index Finger   £5,350 to £7,125

This level is appropriate where a fracture has
mended quickly but grip has remained impaired,
there is pain on heavy use and osteoarthritis is
likely in due course.

(m) Total Loss of Middle Finger   **In the region of £8,900**

(n) Serious Injury to Ring or Middle Fingers   **£8,650 to £9,400**

Fractures or serious injury to tendons causing stiffness, deformity and permanent loss of grip or dexterity will fall within this bracket.

(o) Loss of the Terminal Phalanx of the Ring or Middle Fingers   **£2,300 to £4,575**

(p) Amputation of Little Finger   **£5,100 to £7,125**

(q) Loss of Part of the Little Finger   **£2,300 to £3,450**

This is appropriate where the remaining tip is sensitive.

(r) Amputation of Ring and Little Fingers   **In the region of £12,725**

(s) Amputation of the Terminal Phalanges of the Index and Middle Fingers   **In the region of £14,500**

Such injury will involve scarring, restriction of movement and impairment of grip and fine handling.

(t) Fracture of One Finger   **£1,775 to £2,800**

Depending upon recovery time.

(u) Loss of Thumb   **£20,350 to £32,000**

(v) **Very Serious Injury to Thumb** £11,450 to £20,350

This bracket is appropriate where the thumb has been severed at the base and grafted back leaving a virtually useless and deformed digit, or where the thumb has been amputated through the interphalangeal joint.

(w) **Serious Injury to the Thumb** £7,375 to £9,700

Such injuries may involve amputation of the tip, nerve damage or fracture necessitating the insertion of wires as a result of which the thumb is cold and ultra-sensitive and there is impaired grip and loss of manual dexterity.

(x) **Moderate Injuries to the Thumb** £5,600 to £7,375

These are injuries such as those necessitating arthrodesis of the interphalangeal joint or causing damage to tendons or nerves. Such injuries result in impairment of sensation and function and cosmetic deformity.

(y) **Severe Dislocation of the Thumb** £2,300 to £4,000

(z) **Minor Injuries to the Thumb** In the region of £2,300

Such an injury would be a fracture which has recovered in six months except for residual stiffness and some discomfort.

(aa) **Trivial Thumb Injuries** In the region of £1,250

These may have caused severe pain for a very short time but will have resolved within a few months.

(J) Vibration White Finger (VWF) and/or Hand—Arm Vibration Syndrome (HAVS)

Vibration White Finger and/or Hand—Arm Vibration Syndrome, caused by exposure to vibration, is a slowly progressive condition, the development and severity of which are affected by the degree of exposure, in particular the magnitude, frequency, duration and transmission of the vibration. The symptoms are similar to those experienced in the constitutional condition of Raynaud's phenomenon.

The Stockholm Workshop Scale is now the accepted table for grading the severity of the condition. The Scale classifies both the vascular and sensorineural components in two complementary tables. Individual assessment is made separately for each hand and for each finger. Any interference with work or social life is disregarded.

Accordingly, depending on individual circumstances, a lower award might be made despite significant disablement where, e.g., employment is unaffected, whilst a higher award might be attracted where there is a lesser disability but a consequential inability to pursue working life.

The vascular component is graded between Stage 0 (no attacks) through mild, moderate and severe to 4V (very severe) where there are frequent attacks affecting all phalanges of most fingers with atrophic changes in the fingertips.

The sensorineural component is graded between Stage 0SN (no symptoms) and 3SN (intermittent or persistent numbness, reduced tactile discrimination and/or manipulative dexterity).

The grade of disorder is indicated by the stage and number of affected fingers on both hands.

The assessment of damages depends upon the extent of the symptoms and their impact upon work and social life.

In a severe case, the injury may be regarded as damaging a hand rather than being confined to the fingers.

The brackets can best be defined and valued as follows:

(i)	Most Serious	£18,325 to £22,400
(ii)	Serious	£9,700 to £18,325
(iii)	Moderate	£5,100 to £9,700
(iv)	Minor	£1,775 to £5,100

(K) WORK-RELATED UPPER LIMB DISORDERS

This section covers a range of upper limb injury in the form of the following pathological conditions:

(a) Tenosynovitis: inflammation of synovial sheaths of tendons usually resolving with rest over a short period. Sometimes this condition leads to continuing symptoms of loss of grip and dexterity.

(b) De Quervain's tenosynovitis: a form of tenosynovitis, rarely bilateral, involving inflammation of the tendons of the thumb.

(c) Stenosing tenosynovitis: otherwise, trigger finger/thumb: thickening tendons.

(d) Carpal tunnel syndrome: constriction of the median nerve of the wrist or thickening of surrounding tissue. It is often relieved by a decompression operation.

(e) Epicondylitis: inflammation in the elbow joint: medial = golfer's elbow; lateral = tennis elbow.

The brackets below apply to all these conditions but the level of the award is affected by the following considerations regardless of the precise condition:

(i) are the effects bilateral or one sided?

(ii) the level of symptoms, i.e., pain, swelling, tenderness, crepitus;

(iii) the ability to work;

(iv) the capacity to avoid the recurrence of symptoms;

(v) surgery.

(a) Continuing bilateral disability with surgery and loss of employment. £12,725 to £13,500

(b) Continuing, but fluctuating and unilateral symptoms. £8,650 to £9,400

(c) Symptoms resolving in the course of two years. £5,100 to £5,600

(d) Complete recovery within a short period. £1,300 to £2,000

(L) Leg Injuries

(a) Amputations

(i) Total Loss of Both Legs £140,500 to £165,500

This is the appropriate award where both legs are lost above the knee and particularly if near to the hip leaving one or both stumps less than adequate to accommodate a useful prosthesis.

(ii) **Below-knee Amputation of Both Legs** £117,000 to £157,750

The top of the bracket is appropriate where both legs are amputated just below the knee. Amputations lower down result in a lower award.

(iii) **Above-knee Amputation of One Leg** £56,000 to £81,500

The area within the bracket within which the award should fall will depend upon such factors as the level of the amputation; the severity of phantom pains; whether or not there have been any problems with a prosthesis and any side effects such as depression or backache.

(iv) **Below-knee Amputation of One Leg** £52,950 to £76,350

The straightforward case of a below-knee amputation with no complications would justify an award at the bottom of this bracket. At or towards the top of the range would come the traumatic amputation which occurs in a devastating accident, where the injured person remained fully conscious, or cases where attempts to save the leg led to numerous unsuccessful operations so that amputation occurred years after the event.

(b) **Severe Leg Injuries**

(i) **The Most Serious Injuries Short of Amputation** £56,000 to £79,000

Some injuries, although not involving amputation, are so severe that the courts have awarded damages at a comparable level. Such injuries would include extensive degloving of the leg, where there is gross shortening of the leg or where fractures have not united and extensive bone grafting has been undertaken.

(ii) **Very Serious**   **£32,000 to £49,350**

Injuries leading to permanent problems with mobility, the need for crutches for the remainder of the injured person's life; injuries where multiple fractures have taken years to heal and have led to serious deformity and limitation of movement, or where arthritis has developed in a joint so that further surgical treatment is likely.

(iii) **Serious**   **£22,650 to £32,000**

Serious injuries to joints or ligaments resulting in instability, prolonged treatment, a lengthy period of non-weight-bearing, the near certainty that arthritis will ensue; injuries involving the hip, requiring arthrodesis or hip replacement, extensive scarring. To justify an award within this bracket a combination of such features will generally be necessary.

(iv) **Moderate**   **£16,300 to £22,650**

This bracket includes severe, complicated or multiple fractures. The level of an award within the bracket will be influenced by the period off work; the presence or risk of degenerative changes; imperfect union of fractures, muscle wasting; limited joint movements; instability in the knee; unsightly scarring or permanently increased vulnerability to future damage.

(c) Less Serious Leg Injuries

(i) **Fractures from which an Incomplete Recovery is Made**   **£10,500 to £16,300**

The injured person will be left with a metal implant and/or defective gait, a limp, impaired mobility, sensory loss, discomfort or an exacerbation of a pre-existing disability.

(ii) **Simple Fracture of a Femur with No Damage to Articular Surfaces**   **£5,350 to £8,150**

(iii) **Simple Fractures and Soft Tissue Injuries**   **Up to £5,350**

At the top of the bracket will come simple fractures of the tibia or fibula from which a complete recovery has been made. Below this level fall a wide variety of soft tissue injuries, lacerations, cuts, bruising or contusions, all of which have recovered completely or almost so and any residual disability is cosmetic or of a minor nature.

(M) Knee Injuries

Knee injuries fall within a bracket extending from a few hundred pounds for a simple twisting injury up to £50,000 or so.

(a) Severe

(i) Serious knee injury where there has been disruption of the joint, gross ligamentous damage, lengthy treatment, considerable pain and loss of function and an arthrodesis or arthroplasty has taken place or is inevitable.   **£40,750 to £56,000**

(ii) Leg fracture extending into the knee joint causing pain which is constant, permanent, limiting movement or impairing agility and rendering the injured person prone to osteoarthritis and the risk of arthroplasty.

£30,500 to £40,750

(iii) Less severe injuries than those in (a)(ii) above and/or injuries which result in less severe disability. There may be continuing symptoms by way of pain and discomfort and limitation of movement or instability or deformity with the risk that degenerative changes may occur in the long term as a result of damage to the kneecap, ligamentous or meniscal injury or muscular wasting.

£15,500 to £25,000

(b) Moderate

(i) Injuries involving dislocation, torn cartilage or meniscus or which accelerate symptoms from a pre-existing condition but which additionally result in minor instability, wasting, weakness or other mild future disability.

£8,400 to £15,500

(ii) This bracket includes injuries similar to those in (b)(i) above, but less serious, and also lacerations, twisting or bruising injuries. Where recovery has been complete the award is unlikely to exceed £3,500. Where there is continuous aching or discomfort, or occasional pain, the award will be towards the upper end of the bracket.

Up to £8,150

(N) ANKLE INJURIES

The vast majority of ankle injuries are worth significantly less than £12,500.

(a) Very Severe   £29,000 to £40,750

Examples of injuries falling within this bracket
are limited and unusual. They include cases of a
transmalleolar fracture of the ankle with extensive soft-tissue damage resulting in deformity and
the risk that any future injury to the leg might
necessitate a below-knee amputation, or cases of
bilateral ankle fractures causing degeneration of
the joints at a young age so that arthrodesis is
necessary.

(b) Severe   £18,325 to £29,000

Injuries necessitating an extensive period of
treatment and/or a lengthy period in plaster or
where pins and plates have been inserted and
there is significant residual disability in the form
of ankle instability, severely limited ability to
walk. The level of the award within the bracket
will be determined in part by such features as a
failed arthrodesis, regular sleep disturbance, unsightly scarring and any need to wear special
footwear.

(c) Moderate   £7,625 to £15,500

Fractures, ligamentous tears and the like which
give rise to less serious disabilities such as difficulty in walking on uneven ground, awkward-
ness on stairs, irritation from metal plates and
residual scarring.

(d) Modest Injuries   Up to £8,150

The less serious, minor or undisplaced fractures,
sprains and ligamentous injuries. The level of the
award within the bracket will be determined by
whether or not a complete recovery has been
made and, if recovery is incomplete, whether

there is any tendency for the ankle to give way, and whether there is scarring, aching or discomfort or the possibility of later osteoarthritis.

Where recovery is within a year, the award is unlikely to exceed £3,300.

(O) Achilles Tendon

(a) Most Serious   In the region of £22,900

Severance of the tendon and the peroneus longus muscle giving rise to cramp, swelling and restricted ankle movement necessitating the cessation of active sports.

(b) Serious   £14,500 to £17,550

Where complete division of the tendon has been successfully repaired but there is residual weakness, a limitation of ankle movements, a limp and residual scarring and where further improvement is unlikely.

(c) Moderate   £8,650 to £10,500

Complete division of the tendon but where its repair has left no significant functional disability.

(d) Minor   £4,300 to £5,850

A turning of the ankle resulting in some damage to the tendon and a feeling of being unsure of ankle support.

(P) Foot Injuries

(a) Amputation of Both Feet   £98,500 to £117,000

This injury is treated similarly to below-knee amputation of both legs because the common feature is loss of a useful ankle joint.

(b) Amputation of One Foot   £48,850 to £63,625

This injury is also treated as similar to a below-knee amputation because of the loss of the ankle joint.

(c) Very Severe   £48,850 to £63,625

To fall within this bracket the injury must produce permanent and severe pain or really serious permanent disability. Examples would include the traumatic amputation of the forefoot where there was a significant risk of the need for a full amputation and serious exacerbation of an existing back problem, or cases of the loss of a substantial portion of the heel so that mobility was grossly restricted.

(d) Severe   £26,500 to £39,200

Fractures of *both* heels or feet with a substantial restriction on mobility or considerable or permanent pain. The bracket will also include unusually severe injury to a single foot resulting, for example, in heel fusion, osteoporosis, ulceration or other disability preventing the wearing of ordinary shoes. It will also apply in the case of a drop foot deformity corrected by a brace.

(e) **Serious**   **£14,500 to £22,650**

Towards the top end of the bracket fall cases such
as those of grievous burns to both feet requiring
multiple operations and leaving disfiguring scars
and persistent irritation. At the lower end of the
bracket would be those injuries less severe than
in (d) above but leading to fusion of foot
joints, continuing pain from traumatic arthritis,
prolonged treatment and the future risk of
osteoarthritis.

(f) **Moderate**   **£8,150 to £14,500**

Displaced metatarsal fractures resulting in permanent deformity and continuing symptoms.

(g) **Modest**   **Up to £8,150**

Simple metatarsal fractures, ruptured ligaments,
puncture wounds and the like. Where there are
continuing symptoms, such as a permanent
limp, pain or aching, awards between £4,000 and
£8,150 would be appropriate. Straightforward
foot injuries such as fractures, lacerations, contusions etc. from which complete or near complete recovery is made would justify awards of
£4,000 or less.

(Q) TOE INJURIES

(a) **Amputation of All Toes**   **£21,350 to £32,800**

The position within the bracket will be determined by, for example, whether or not the
amputation was traumatic or surgical and the
extent of the loss of the forefoot together with
the residual effects on mobility.

(b) **Amputation of the Great Toe**   **In the region of £18,325**

(c) **Severe Toe Injuries**   **£8,150 to £11,200**

This is the appropriate bracket for severe crush injuries, falling short of the need for amputation or necessitating only partial amputation. It also includes bursting wounds and injuries resulting in severe damage and in any event producing significant continuing symptoms.

(d) **Serious Toe Injuries**   **£5,600 to £8,150**

Such injuries will be serious injuries to the great toe or crush and multiple fractures of two or more toes. There will be some permanent disability by way of discomfort, pain or sensitive scarring to justify an award within this bracket. Where there have been a number of unsuccessful operations or persisting stabbing pains, impaired gait or the like the award will tend towards the top end of the bracket.

(e) **Moderate Toe Injuries**   **Up to £5,600**

These injuries include relatively straightforward fractures or the exacerbation of a pre-existing degenerative condition. Only £3,300 or less would be awarded for straightforward fractures of one or more toes with complete resolution within a short period of time and less still for minor injuries involving lacerations, cuts, contusions and bruises, in respect of all of which there would have been a complete or near complete recovery.

7

Facial Injuries

The assessment of general damages for facial injuries is an extremely difficult task, there being three elements which complicate the award.

First, while in most of the cases dealt with below the injuries described are skeletal, many of them will involve an element of disfigurement or at least some cosmetic effect.

Second, in cases where there is a cosmetic element the courts have invariably drawn a distinction between the awards of damages to males and females, the latter attracting the higher awards.

Third, in cases of disfigurement there may also be severe psychological reactions which put the total award at the top of the bracket, or above it altogether.

The subject of burns is not dealt with separately. Burns of any degree of severity are particularly painful and disfiguring, and awards are invariably at the upper ends of the brackets, or above them altogether. The very worst burns may lead not only to considerable disfigurement and pain but to a variety of continuing physical and psychological injuries meriting very high awards.

(A) Skeletal Injuries

(a) Le Fort Fractures of Frontal Facial Bones

£14,000 to £21,350

(b) Multiple Fractures of Facial Bones

£8,650 to £14,000

Involving some facial deformity of a permanent nature.

(c) Fractures of Nose or Nasal Complex

(i) Serious or multiple fractures requiring a number of operations and/or resulting in permanent damage to airways and/or nerves or tear ducts and/or facial deformity.

£6,100 to £13,500

(ii) Displaced fracture where recovery complete but only after surgery.

£2,300 to £3,000

(iii) Displaced fracture requiring no more than manipulation.

£1,400 to £1,775

(iv) Simple undisplaced fracture with full recovery.

£1,000 to £1,400

(d) Fractures of Cheekbones

(i) Serious fractures requiring surgery but with lasting consequences such as paraesthesia in the cheeks or the lips or some element of disfigurement.

£5,850 to £9,150

(ii) Simple fracture of cheekbones for which some reconstructive surgery is necessary but from which there is a complete recovery with no or only minimal cosmetic effects.

£2,550 to £3,800

(iii)	Simple fracture of cheekbone for which no surgery is required and where a complete recovery is effected.	£1,400 to £1,725

(e) Fractures of Jaws

(i)	Very serious multiple fractures followed by prolonged treatment and permanent consequences, including severe pain, restriction in eating, paraesthesia and/or the risk of arthritis in the joints.	£17,800 to £26,500
(ii)	Serious fracture with permanent consequences such as difficulty in opening the mouth or with eating or where there is paraesthesia in the area of the jaw.	£10,500 to £17,800
(iii)	Simple fracture requiring immobilisation but from which recovery is complete.	£3,800 to £5,100

(f) Damage to Teeth

In these cases there will generally have been a course of treatment as a result of the initial injury. The amounts awarded will vary according to the extent and/or the degree of discomfort of such treatment. Any difficulty with eating increases the award. These cases may overlap with fractures of the jaw, meriting awards in the brackets for such fractures. Awards may be greater where the damage results in or is caused by protracted dentistry.

(i)	Loss of or serious damage to several front teeth.	£5,100 to £6,600
(ii)	Loss of or serious damage to two front teeth.	£2,550 to £4,300
(iii)	Loss of or serious damage to one front tooth.	£1,300 to £2,300

(iv)   Loss of or damage to back teeth: per tooth: **£630 to £1,000**

(B) Facial Disfigurement

In this class of case the distinction between male and female and the subjective approach are of particular significance. Larger awards than those indicated may be justified if there have been many operations.

(a) Females

(i)   **Very Severe Scarring**   **£28,000 to £56,500**

In a relatively young woman (teens to early 30s) where the cosmetic effect is very disfiguring and the psychological reaction severe.

(ii)   **Less Severe Scarring**   **£17,550 to £28,000**

Where the disfigurement is still substantial and where there is a significant psychological reaction.

(iii)   **Significant Scarring**   **£10,500 to £17,550**

Where the worst effects have been or will be reduced by plastic surgery leaving some cosmetic disability and where the psychological reaction is not great or, having been considerable at the outset, has diminished to relatively minor proportions.

(iv)   **Less Significant Scarring**   **£2,300 to £8,150**

In these cases there may be but one scar which can be camouflaged or, though there is a number of very small scars, the overall effect is to mar but not markedly to affect the appearance and the reaction is no more than that of an ordinarily sensitive young woman.

(v)   Trivial Scarring   £1,000 to £2,000

In these cases the effect is minor only.

(b) Males

(i)   Very Severe Scarring   £17,550 to £38,175

These are to be found especially in males under 30, where there is permanent disfigurement even after plastic surgery and a considerable element of psychological reaction.

(ii)   Less Severe Scarring   £10,500 to £17,550

This will have left moderate to severe permanent disfigurement.

(iii)   Significant Scarring   £5,350 to £10,500

Such scars will remain visible at conversational distances.

(iv)   Less Significant Scarring   £2,300 to £5,350

Such scarring is not particularly prominent except on close inspection.

(v)   Trivial Scarring   £1,000 to £2,000

In these cases the effect is minor only.

8

Scarring to Other Parts of the Body

This is an area in which it is not possible to offer much useful guidance. The principles are the same as those applied to cases of facial disfigurement. It must be remembered that many of the physical injuries already described involve some element of disfigurement and that element is of course taken into account in suggesting the appropriate bracket. There remain some cases where the element of disfigurement is the predominant one in the assessment of damages. Where the scarring is not to the face or is not usually visible then the awards will tend to be lower than those for facial or readily visible disfigurement.

A large proportion of awards for a number of noticeable laceration scars, or a single disfiguring scar, of leg(s) or arm(s) or hand(s) or back or chest (male), fall in the bracket of £4,500 to £8,200.

In cases where an exploratory laparotomy has been performed but no significant internal injury has been found, the award for the operation and the inevitable scar is in the region of £5,000.

A single noticeable scar, or several superficial scars, of leg(s) or arm(s) or hand(s), with some minor cosmetic deficit justifies £1,300 to £2,300.

As we have noted in Chapter 7, the effects of burns will normally be regarded as more serious since they tend to cause a greater degree of pain and may lead to continuing physical and psychological injury.

9

Damage to Hair

(a) Damage to hair in consequence of defective permanent waving, tinting or the like, where the effects are dermatitis or tingling or 'burning' of the scalp causing dry, brittle hair, which breaks off and/or falls out, leading to distress, depression, embarrassment and loss of confidence, and inhibiting social life. In the more serious cases thinning continues and the prospects of regrowth are poor or there has been total loss of areas of hair and regrowth is slow.

£4,300 to £6,350

There may be a larger award in cases of psychological disability.

(b) Less serious versions of the above where symptoms are fewer or only of a minor character; also, cases where hair has been pulled out leaving bald patches. The level of the award will depend on the length of time taken before regrowth occurs.

£2,300 to £4,300

10

Dermatitis

Apart from dermatitis of the scalp (see Chapter 9), most of the reported cases relate to dermatitis of the hands.

(a) Dermatitis of both hands, with cracking and soreness, affecting employment and domestic capability, possibly with some psychological consequences, lasting for some years, perhaps indefinitely.   **£8,150 to £11,200**

(b) Dermatitis of both hands, continuing for a significant period, but settling with treatment and/or use of gloves for specific tasks.   **£5,100 to £6,600**

(c) Itching, irritation of and/or rashes on one or both hands, but resolving within a few months with treatment.   **£1,000 to £2,300**

Index